CW00544704

Fragments Of Ancient Poetry

James MacPherson

Table of Contents

Fragments Of Ancient Poetry

James MacPherson

Kessinger Publishing reprints thousands of hard–to–find books!

Visit us at http://www.kessinger.net

Introduction by JOHN J. DUNN

GENERAL EDITORS

George Robert Guffey, University of California, Los Angeles

Earl Miner, University of California, Los Angeles

Maximillian E. Novak, University of California, Los Angeles

Robert Vosper, William Andrews Clark Memorial Library

ADVISORY EDITORS

Richard C. Boys, University of Michigan

James L. Clifford, Columbia University

Ralph Cohen, University of California, Los Angeles

Vinton A. Dearing, University of California, Los Angeles

Arthur Friedman, University of Chicago

Louis A. Landa, Princeton University

Samuel H. Monk, University of Minnesota

Everett T. Moore, University of California, Los Angeles

Lawrence Clark Powell, William Andrews Clark Memorial Library

James Sutherland, University College, London

H. T. Swedenberg, Jr., University of California, Los Angeles

CORRESPONDING SECRETARY

Edna C. Davis, William Andrews Clark Memorial Library

INTRODUCTION

Byron was actually the third Scotsman in about fifty years who awoke and found himself famous; the sudden rise from obscurity to international fame had been experienced earlier by two fellow countrymen, Sir Walter Scott and James Macpherson. Considering the greatness of the reputation of the two younger writers, it may seem strange to link their names with Macpherson's, but in the early nineteenth century it would not have seemed so odd. In fact, as young men both Scott and Byron would have probably have been flattered by such an association. Scott tells us that in his youth he "devoured rather than perused" Ossian and that he could repeat whole duans "without remorse"; and, as I shall discuss later, Byron paid Macpherson the high compliment of writing an imitation of Ossian, which he published in *Hours of Idleness.*

The publication of the modest and anonymous pamphlet, *Fragments of Ancient Poetry* marks the beginning of Macpherson's rise to fame, and concomitantly the start of a controversy that is unique in literary history. For the half–century that followed, the body of poetry that was eventually collected as *The Poems of Ossian* provoked the comment of nearly every important man of letters. Extravagance and partisanship were characteristic of most of the remarks, but few literary men were indifferent.

The intensity and duration of the controversy are indicative of how seriously Macpherson's work was taken, for it was to many readers of the day daring, original, and passionate. Even Malcolm Laing, whose ardor in exposing Macpherson's imposture exceeded that of Dr. Johnson, responded to the literary quality of the poems. In a note on the fourth and fifth "Fragments" the arch prosecutor of Macpherson commented,

"From a singular coincidence of circumstances, it was in this house, where I now write, that I first read the poems in my early youth, with an ardent credulity that remained unshaken for many years of my life; and with a pleasure to which even the triumphant satisfaction of detecting the imposture is comparatively nothing. The enthusiasm with which I read and studied the poems, enabled me afterwards, when my suspicions were once awakened, to trace and expose the deception with greater success. Yet, notwithstanding the severity of minute criticism, I can still peruse them as a wild and wonderful assemblage of imitation with which the fancy is often pleased and gratified, even when the judgment condemns them most."[2]

II

It was John Home, famous on both sides of the Tweed as the author of *Douglas*, who first encouraged Macpherson to undertake his translations. While taking the waters at Moffat in the fall of 1759, he was pleased to meet a young Highland tutor, who was not only familiar with ancient Gaelic poetry but who had in his possession several such poems. Home, like nearly all of the Edinburgh literati, knew no Gaelic and asked Macpherson to translate one of them. The younger man at first protested that a translation "would give a very imperfect idea of the original," but Home "with some difficulty" persuaded him to try. In a "day or two" Macpherson brought him the poem that was to become "Fragment VII" in this collection; Home was so much pleased with it that he requested additional translations.[3]

"Jupiter" Carlyle, whose autobiography reflects the keen interest that he took in literature, arrived at Moffat after Home had seen the "translations." Home, he found, "had been highly delighted with them," and when Carlyle read them he "was perfectly astonished at the poetical genius" that they displayed. They agreed that "it was a precious discovery, and that as soon as possible it should be published to the world."[4]

When Home left Moffat he took his find to Edinburgh and showed the translations to the men who earned the city Smollett's sobriquet, a "hotbed of genius": Robertson, fresh from the considerable success of his two volume *History of Scotland* (1759); Robert Fergusson, recently appointed professor of natural history at the University of Edinburgh; Lord Elibank, a learned aristocrat, who had been patron to Home and Robertson; and Hugh Blair, famous for the sermons that he delivered as rector of the High Church of St. Giles. Home was gratified that these men were "no less pleased" with Macpherson's work than he had been. David Hume and David Dalrymple (later Lord Hailes) were soon apprised of the discovery and joined in the chorus of approbation that emanated from the Scottish capitol.

Blair became the spokesman and the leader for the Edinburgh literati, and for the next forty years he lavished his energy in praising and defending Macpherson's work. The translations came to him at the time that he was writing his lectures on *belles lettres* and was thus in the process of formulating his theories on the origins of poetry and the nature of the sublime. Blair lost no time in communicating with Macpherson:

"I being as much struck as Mr Home with the high spirit of poetry which breathed in them, presently made inquiry where Mr. Macpherson was to be found; and having sent for him to come to me, had much conversation with him on the subject."[Footnote 5]

Macpherson told Blair that there were "greater and more considerable poems of the same strain" still extant in the Highlands; Blair like Home was eager for more, but Macpherson again declined to translate them. He said that he felt himself inadequate to render "the spirit and force" of the originals and that "they would be very ill relished by the public as so very different from the strain of modern ideas, and of modern, connected, and polished poetry." This whetted Blair's interest even more, and after "repeated importunity" he persuaded Macpherson to translate more fragments. The result was the present volume, which Blair saw to the press and for which he wrote the Preface "in consequence of the conversations" that he had with Macpherson.[Footnote 6:]

Most of Blair's Preface does seem to be based on information supplied by Macpherson, for Blair had almost no first–hand knowledge about Highland poetry or its traditions. It is apparent from the Preface then, that Macpherson had not yet decided to ascribe the poems to a single poet; Ossian is one of the principal poets in the collection but the whole is merely ascribed "to the bards" (see pp. v–vi). It is also evident from the Preface that Macpherson was shifting from the reluctant "translator" of a few "fragments" to the projector of a full–length epic "if enough encouragement were given for such an undertaking."

Since Blair became famous for his *Critical Dissertation on the Poems of Ossian* (London, 1763), it may seem strange that in the Preface to the *Fragments* he declined to say anything of the "poetical merit" of the collection. The frank adulation of the longer essay, which concludes with the brave assertion that Ossian may be placed "among those whose works are to last for ages,"[7] was partially a reflection of the enthusiasm that greeted each of Macpherson's successive publications.

III

Part of the appeal of the *Fragments* was obviously based on the presumption that they were, as Blair hastened to assure the reader, "genuine remains of ancient Scottish poetry," and therefore provided a remarkable insight into a remote, primitive culture; here were maidens and warriors who lived in antiquity on the harsh, wind–swept wastes of the Highlands, but they were capable of highly refined and sensitive expressions of grief—they were the noblest savages of them all. For some readers the rumors of imposture served to dampen their initial enthusiasm, and such was the case with Hume, Walpole, and Boswell, but many of the admirers of the poems found them rapturous, authentic or not.

After Gray had read several of the "Fragments" in manuscript he wrote to Thomas Warton that he had "gone mad about them"; he added,

> "I was so struck, so *extasie* with their infinite beauty, that
> I writ into Scotland to make a thousand enquiries....
> The whole external evidence would make one believe
> these fragments (for so he calls them, tho' nothing can
> be more entire) counterfeit: but the internal is so strong
> on the other side, that I am resolved to believe them genuine
> spite of the Devil &the Kirk."

Gray concluded his remarks with the assertion that "this Man is the very Demon of Poetry, or he has lighted on a treasure hid for ages."[8]

Nearly fifty years later Byron wrote a "humble imitation" of Ossian for the admirers of Macpherson's work and presented it as evidence of his "attachment to their favorite author," even though he was aware of the imposture. In a note to "The Death of Calmar and Orla," he commented,

"I fear Laing's late edition has completely overthrown every hope that Macpherson's Ossian might prove the translation of a series of poems complete in themselves; but while the imposture is discovered, the merit of the work remains undisputed, though not without faults—particularly, in some parts, turgid and bombastic diction."[9]

In 1819 Hazlitt felt that Ossian is "a feeling and a name that can never be destroyed in the minds of his readers," and he classed the work as one of the four prototypes of poetry along with the Bible, Homer, and Dante. On the question of authenticity he observed,

"If it were indeed possible to shew that this writer was nothing, it would be another instance of mutability, another blank made, another void left in the heart, another confirmation of that feeling which makes him so often complain, 'Roll on, ye dark brown years, ye bring no joy on your wing to Ossian!'"[10]

There is some justice in Macpherson's wry assertion that "those who have doubted my veracity have paid a compliment to my genius."[11] By examining briefly the distinctive form of the "Fragments," their diction, their setting, their tone, and their structure, we may sense something of the qualities of the poems that made them attractive to such men as Gray, Byron, and Hazlitt.

IV

Perhaps Macpherson's most important innovation was to cast his work into what his contemporaries called "measured prose," and it was recognized early that this new form contributed greatly to their appeal. In discussing the *Fragments*, Ramsey of Ochtertyre commented,

"Nothing could be more happy or judicious than his translating in measured prose; for had he attempted it in verse, much of the spirit of the original would have evaporated, supposing him to have had talents and industry to perform that very arduous task upon a great scale. This small publication drew the attention of the literary world to a new species of poetry."[12]

For his new species of poetry Macpherson drew upon the stylistic techniques of the King James Version of the Bible, just as Blake and Whitman were to do later. As Bishop Lowth was the first to point out, parallelism is the basic structural technique. Macpherson incorporated two principal forms of parallelism in his poems: *repetition*, a pattern in which the second line nearly restates the sense of the first, and *completion* in which the second line picks up part of the sense of the first line and adds to it. These are both common in the *Fragments*, but a few examples may be useful. I have rearranged the following lines and in the other passages relating to the structure of the poems in order to call attention to the binary quality of Macpherson's verse:

Repetition

Who can reach the source of thy race, O Connal? And who recount thy Fathers? ("Fragment V")

Oscur my son came down; The mighty in battle descended. ("Fragment VI")

Oscur stood forth to meet him; My son would meet the foe. ("Fragment VIII")

Future times shall hear of thee; They shall hear of the fallen Morar. ("Fragment XII")

Completion

What voice is that I hear? That voice like the summer wind. ("Fragment I")

  The warriors saw her, and loved;
  Their souls were fixed on the maid.
  Each loved her, as his fame;
  Each must possess her or die.
  But her soul was fixed on Oscur;
  My son was the youth of her love. ("Fragment VII")

Macpherson also used grammatical parallelism as a structural device; a series of simple sentences is often used to describe a landscape:

  Autumn is dark on the mountains;
  Grey mist rests on the hills.
  The whirlwind is heard on the heath.
  Dark rolls the river through the narrow plain. ("Fragment V")

The poems also have a discernible rhythmical pattern; the tendency of the lines to form pairs is obvious enough when there is semantic or grammatical parallelism, but there is a general binary pattern throughout. Typically, the first unit is a simple sentence, the

8

second almost any grammatical structure—an appositive, a prepositional phrase, a participle, the second element of a compound verb, a dependent clause. A simile—in grammatical terms, an adverbial phrase—sometimes constitutes the second element. These pairs are often balanced roughly by the presence of two, three, or four accents in each constituent; there are a large number of imbedded iambic and anapestic feet, which give the rhythm an ascending quality:

The da/ughter of R/inval was n/ear;

Crim/ora, br/ight in the arm/our of m/an;

Her ha/ir loose beh/ind,

Her b/ow in her h/and.

She f/ollowed the y/outh to w/ar,

Co/nnal her m/uch bel/oved.

She dr/ew the st/ring on D/argo;

But e/rring pi/erced her C/onnal. ("Fragment V")

As E. H. W. Meyerstein pointed out, "Macpherson can, without extravagance, be regarded as the main originator (after the translators of the Authorized Version) of what's known as 'free verse.'"[13] Macpherson's work certainly served to stimulate prosodic experimentation during the next half century; it is certainly no coincidence that two of the boldest innovators, Blake and Coleridge, were admirers of Macpherson's work.

Macpherson's diction must have also appealed to the growing taste for poetry that was less ornate and studied. His practice was to use a large number of concrete monosyllabic words of Anglo–Saxon origin to describe objects and forces common to rural life. A simple listing of the common nouns from the opening of "Fragment I" will serve to illustrate this tendency: *love, son, hill, deer, dogs, bow–string, wind, stream, rushes, mist, oak, friends.* Such diction bears an obvious kinship to what was to become the staple diction of the romantic lyric; for example, a similar listing from "A Slumber Did

9

My Spirit Seal" would be this: *slumber, spirit, fears, thing, touch, years, motion, force, course, rocks, stones, trees.*

The untamed power of Macpherson's wild natural settings is also striking. Samuel H. Monk has made the point well:

"Ossian's strange exotic wildness and his obscure, terrible glimpses of scenery were in essence something quite new.... Ossian's images were far from "nature methodized." His imagination illumined fitfully a scene of mountains and blasted heaths, as artificially wild as his heroines were artificially sensitive; to modern readers they resemble too much the stage–settings of melodrama. But in 1760, his descriptions carried with them the thrill of the genuine and of naively archaic."

And Monk adds, "imperceptibly the Ossianic poems contributed toward converting Britons, nay, Europeans, into enthusiastic admirers of nature in her wilder moments."[14]

Ghosts are habitually present in the poems, and Macpherson is able to present them convincingly because they are described by a poet who treats them as though they were part of his and his audience's habitual experience. The supernatural world is so familiar, in fact, that it can be used to describe the natural; thus Minvane in "Fragment VII" is called as fair "as the spirits of the hill when at silent noon they glide along the heath." As Patricia M. Spacks has observed, the supernatural seems to be a "genuine part of the poetic texture"; and she adds that

"within this poetic context, the supernatural seems convincing because believed in: it is part of the fabric of life for the characters of the poem. Ghosts in the Ossianic poems, almost uniquely in the mid–eighteenth century, seem genuinely to belong; to this particular poetic conception the supernatural does not seem extraneous."[15]

The *Fragments* was also a cause and a reflection of the rising appeal of the hero of sensibility, whose principal characteristic was that he could feel more intensely than the mass of humanity. The most common emotion that these acutely empathetic heroes felt was grief, the emotion that permeates the *Fragments* and the rest of Macpherson's work. It was the exquisite sensibility of Macpherson's heroes and heroines that the young Goethe was struck by; Werther, an Ossianic hero in his own way, comments,

"You should see what a silly figure I cut when she is mentioned in society! And then if I am even asked how I like her—Like! I hate that word like death. What sort of person must that be who likes Lotte, in whom all senses, all emotions are not completely filled up by her! Like! Recently someone asked me how I like Ossian!"[16]

That Macpherson chose to call his poems "fragments" is indicative of another quality that made them unusual in their day. The poems have a spontaneity that is suggested by the fact that the poets seem to be creating their songs as the direct reflection of an emotional experience. In contrast to the image of the poet as the orderer, the craftsman, the poets of the *Fragments* have a kind of artlessness (to us a very studied one, to be sure) that gave them an aura of sincerity and honesty. The poems are fragmentary in the sense that they do not follow any orderly, rational plan but seem to take the form that corresponds to the development of an emotional experience. As Macpherson told Blair they are very different from "modern, connected, and polished poetry."

V

The *Fragments* proved an immediate success and Macpherson's Edinburgh patrons moved swiftly to raise enough money to enable the young Highlander to resign his position as tutor and to devote himself to collecting and translating the Gaelic poetry still extant in the Highlands. Blair recalled that he and Lord Elibank were instrumental in convening a dinner meeting that was attended by "many of the first persons of rank and taste in Edinburgh," including Robertson, Home, and Fergusson.[17] Robert Chalmers acted as treasurer; among the forty odd subscribers who contributed 60L, were James Boswell and David Hume.[18] By the time of the second edition of the *Fragments* (also in 1760), Blair, or more likely Macpherson himself, could inform the public in the "Advertisement" "that measures are now taken for making a full collection of the remaining Scottish bards; in particular, for recovering and translating the heroic poem mentioned in the preface."

Macpherson, a frugal man, included many of the "Fragments" in his later work. Sometimes he introduced them into the notes as being later than Ossian but in the same spirit; at other times he introduced them as episodes in the longer narratives. With the exception of Laing's edition, they are not set off, however, and anyone who wishes to see what caused the initial Ossianic fervor must consult the original volume.

When we have to remind ourselves that a work of art was revolutionary in its day, we can be sure that we are dealing with something closer to cultural artifact than to art, and it must be granted that this is true of Macpherson's work; nevertheless, the fact that Ossian aroused the interest of major men of letters for fifty years is suggestive of his importance as an innovator. In a curious way, Macpherson's achievement has been overshadowed by the fact that many greater writers followed him and developed the artistic direction that he was among the first to take.

NOTES TO THE INTRODUCTION

[1] See Scott's letter to Anna Seward in J. G. Lockhart, *Memoirs of Sir Walter Scott* (London, 1900), I, 410–15.

[2] *The Poems of Ossian*, ed. Malcolm Laing (Edinburgh, 1805), I, 441.

[3] See Home's letter to Mackenzie in the *Report of the Committee of the Highland Society of Scotland* (Edinburgh, 1805), Appendix, pp. 68–69.

[4] Carlyle to Mackenzie, *ibid.*, p. 66.

[5] Blair to Mackenzie, *ibid.*, p. 57.

[6] *Ibid.*, p. 58.

[7] Quoted from *The Poems of Ossian* (London, 1807), I, 222. After its initial separate publication, Blair's dissertation was regularly included with the collected poems.

[8] *Correspondence of Thomas Gray*, ed. Paget Toynbee and Leonard Whibley (Oxford, 1935), II, 679–80.

[9] *The Works of Lord Byron, Poetry*, ed. Ernest Hartley Coleridge (London, 1898), I, 183.

[10] "On Poetry in General," *The Complete Works of William Hazlitt*, ed. P. P. Howe (London, 1930), V, 18.

[11] Quoted in Henry Grey Graham, *Scottish Men of Letters in the Eighteenth Century* (London, 1908), p. 240.

[12] *Scotland and Scotsmen in the Eighteenth Century*, ed. Alexander Allardyce (Edinburgh, 1888), I, 547.

[13] "The Influence of Ossian," *English*, VII (1948), 96.

[14] *The Sublime* (Ann Arbor, 1960), p. 126.

[15] *The Insistence of Horror* (Cambridge, Mass., 1962), pp. 86–87.

[16] *The Sufferings of Young Werther*, trans. Bayard Morgan (New York, 1957), p. 51.

17 *Report*, Appendix, p. 58.

18 See Robert M. Schmitz, *Hugh Blair* (New York, 1948), p. 48.

FRAGMENTS OF ANCIENT POETRY

Collected in the Highlands of Scotland,

AND

Translated from the Galic or Erse Language

"Vos quoque qui fortes animas, belloque peremtas
Laudibus in longum vates dimittitis aevuin,
Plurima securi fudistis carmina *Bardi*."

LUCAN

PREFACE

The public may depend on the following fragments as genuine remains of
ancient Scottish poetry. The date of their composition cannot be exactly
ascertained. Tradition, in the country where they were written, refers
them to an aera of the most remote antiquity: and this tradition is
supported by the spirit and strain of the poems themselves; which abound
with those ideas, and paint those manners, that belong to the most early
state of society. The diction too, in the original, is very obsolete;
and differs widely from the style of such poems as have been written in
the same language two or three centuries ago. They were certainly
composed before the establishment of clanship in the northern part of
Scotland, which is itself very ancient; for had clans been then formed
and known, they must have made a considerable figure in the work of a
Highland Bard; whereas there is not the least mention of them in these
poems. It is remarkable that there are found in them no allusions to the
Christian religion or worship; indeed, few traces of religion of any kind.
One circumstance seems to prove them to be coeval with the very infancy
of Christianity in Scotland. In a fragment of the same poems, which the
translator has seen, a Culdee or Monk is represented as desirous to take
down in writing from the mouth of Oscian, who is the principal personage
in several of the following fragments, his warlike atchievements and

14

those of his family. But Oscian treats the monk and his religion with
disdain, telling him, that the deeds of such great men were subjects too
high to be recorded by him, or by any of his religion: A full proof that
Christianity was not as yet established in the country.

Though the poems now published appear as detached pieces in this
collection, there is ground to believe that most of them were originally
episodes of a greater work which related to the wars of Fingal.
Concerning this hero innumerable traditions remain, to this day, in the
Highlands of Scotland. The story of Oscian, his son, is so generally
known, that to describe one in whom the race of a great family ends, it
has passed into a proverb; "Oscian the last of the heroes."

There can be no doubt that these poems are to be ascribed to the Bards;
a race of men well known to have continued throughout many ages in
Ireland and the north of Scotland. Every chief or great man had in his
family a Bard or poet, whose office it was to record in verse, the
illustrious actions of that family. By the succession of these Bards, such
poems were handed down from race to race; some in manuscript, but more by
oral tradition. And tradition, in a country so free of intermixture with
foreigners, and among a people so strongly attached to the memory of their
ancestors, has preserved many of them in a great measure incorrupted to
this day.

They are not set to music, nor sung. The verification in the original is
simple; and to such as understand the language, very smooth and beautiful;
Rhyme is seldom used: but the cadence, and the length of the line varied,
so as to suit the sense. The translation is extremely literal. Even the
arrangement of the words in the original has been imitated; to which must
be imputed some inversions in the style, that otherwise would not have
been chosen.

Of the poetical merit of these fragments nothing shall here be said. Let
the public judge, and pronounce. It is believed, that, by a careful
inquiry, many more remains of ancient genius, no less valuable than those
now given to the world, might be found in the same country where these

have been collected. In particular there is reason to hope that one work
of considerable length, and which deserves to be styled an heroic poem,
might be recovered and translated, if encouragement were given to such an
undertaking. The subject is, an invasion of Ireland by Swarthan King of
Lochlyn; which is the name of Denmark in the Erse language. Cuchulaid,
the General or Chief of the Irish tribes, upon intelligence of the
invasion, assembles his forces. Councils are held; and battles fought.
But after several unsuccescful engagements, the Irish are forced to
submit. At length, Fingal King of Scotland, called in this poem, "The
Desert of the hills," arrives with his ships to assist Cuchulaid. He
expels the Danes from the country; and returns home victorious. This poem
is held to be of greater antiquity than any of the rest that are preserved.
And the author speaks of himself as present in the expedition of Fingal.
The three last poems in the collection are fragments which the translator
obtained of this epic poem; and though very imperfect, they were judged not
unworthy of being inserted. If the whole were recovered, it might serve to
throw confiderable light upon the Scottish and Irish antiquities.

FRAGMENT

I

SHILRIC, VINVELA.

VINVELA

My love is a son of the hill.
He pursues the flying deer.
His grey dogs are panting
around him; his bow-string sounds in

the wind. Whether by the fount of
the rock, or by the stream of the
mountain thou liest; when the rushes are
nodding with the wind, and the mist
is flying over thee, let me approach
my love unperceived, and see him
from the rock. Lovely I saw thee
first by the aged oak; thou wert returning
tall from the chace; the fairest
among thy friends.

SHILRIC.

What voice is that I hear? that
voice like the summer–wind.—I sit
not by the nodding rushes; I hear not
the fount of the rock. Afar, Vinvela,
afar I go to the wars of Fingal. My
dogs attend me no more. No more
I tread the hill. No more from on
high I see thee, fair–moving by the
stream of the plain; bright as the
bow of heaven; as the moon on the
western wave.

VINVELA.

Then thou art gone, O Shilric!
and I am alone on the hill. The
deer are seen on the brow; void of
fear they graze along. No more they
dread the wind; no more the rustling
tree. The hunter is far removed;
he is in the field of graves. Strangers!
sons of the waves! spare my
lovely Shilric.

SHILRIC.

If fall I must in the field, raise high
my grave, Vinvela. Grey stones, and
heaped-up earth, shall murk me to future
times. When the hunter shall sit by
the mound, and produce his food at
noon, "some warrior rests here," he
will say; and my fame shall live in his
praise. Remember me, Vinvela, when
low on earth I lie!

VINVELA.

Yes!—I will remember thee—indeed
my Shilric will fall. What shall I do,
my love! when thou art gone for ever?
Through these hills I will go at noon: O
will go through the silent heath. There
I will see where often thou sattest returning
from the chace. Indeed, my Shilric
will fall; but I will remember
him.

II

I sit by the mossy fountain; on the
top of the hill of winds. One tree is
rustling above me. Dark waves roll

18

over the heath. The lake is troubled
below. The deer descend from the
hill. No hunter at a distance is seen;
no whistling cow–herd is nigh. It is
mid–day: but all is silent. Sad are my
thoughts as I sit alone. Didst thou
but appear, O my love, a wanderer on
the heath! thy hair floating on the
wind behind thee; thy bosom heaving
on the sight; thine eyes full of tears
for thy friends, whom the mist of the
hill had concealed! Thee I would comfort,
my love, and bring thee to thy
father's house.

But is it she that there appears, like
a beam of light on the heath? bright
as the moon in autumn, as the sun in
a summer–storm?—She speaks: but
how weak her voice! like the breeze
in the reeds of the pool. Hark!

Returnest thou safe from the war?
"Where are thy friends, my love? I
heard of thy death on the hill; I heard
and mourned thee, Shilric!"

Yes, my fair, I return; but I alone
of my race. Thou shalt see them no
more: their graves I raised on the plain.
But why art thou on the desert hill?
why on the heath, alone?

Alone I am, O Shilric! alone in the
winter–house. With grief for thee I
expired. Shilric, I am pale in the tomb.

She fleets, she sails away; as grey
mist before the wind!—and, wilt thou
not stay, my love? Stay and behold
my tears? fair thou appearest, my love!
fair thou wast, when alive!

By the mossy fountain I will sit; on
the top of the hill of winds. When
mid–day is silent around, converse, O
my love, with me! come on the wings
of the gale! on the blast of the mountain,
come! Let me hear thy voice, as
thou passest, when mid–day is silent around.

III

Evening is grey on the hills. The
north wind resounds through the
woods. White clouds rise on the sky: the
trembling snow descends. The river howls
afar, along its winding course. Sad,
by a hollow rock, the grey–hair'd Carryl
sat. Dry fern waves over his head; his
seat is in an aged birch. Clear to the
roaring winds he lifts his voice of woe.

Tossed on the wavy ocean is He,
the hope of the isles; Malcolm, the
support of the poor; foe to the proud

in arms! Why hast thou left us behind?
why live we to mourn thy fate? We
might have heard, with thee, the voice
of the deep; have seen the oozy rock.

Sad on the sea—beat shore thy spouse
looketh for thy return. The time of
thy promise is come; the night is gathering
around. But no white sail is
on the sea; no voice is heard except
the blustering winds. Low is the soul
of the war! Wet are the locks of youth!
By the foot of some rock thou liest;
washed by the waves as they come.
Why, ye winds, did ye bear him on
the desert rock? Why, ye waves, did
ye roll over him?

But, Oh! what voice is that?
Who rides on that meteor of fire! Green
are his airy limbs. It is he! it is the
ghost of Malcolm!—Rest, lovely soul,
rest on the rock; and let me hear thy
voice!—He is gone, like a dream of
the night. I see him through the trees.
Daughter of Reynold! he is gone.
Thy spouse shall return no more. No
more shall his hounds come from the
hill, forerunners of their master. No
more from the distant rock shall his
voice greet thine ear. Silent is he in
the deep, unhappy daughter of Reynold!

I will sit by the stream of the plain.
Ye rocks! hang over my head. Hear
my voice, ye trees! as ye bend on the

shaggy hill. My voice shall preserve
the praise of him, the hope of the
isles.

IV

CONNAL, CRIMORA,

CRIMORA.

Who cometh from the hill, like
a cloud tinged with the beam
of the west? Whose voice is that, loud
as the wind, but pleasant as the harp of
Carryl? It is my love in the light of
steel; but sad is his darkened brow.
Live the mighty race of Fingal? or
what disturbs my Connal?

CONNAL.

They live. I saw them return from
the chace, like a stream of light. The
sun was on their shields: In a line they
descended the hill. Loud is the voice of
the youth; the war, my love, is near.
To—morrow the enormous Dargo comes
to try the force of our race. The race of
Fingal he defies; the race of battle and
wounds.

CRIMORA.

Connal, I saw his sails like grey mist
on the sable wave. They came to land.
Connnal, many are the warriors of
Dargo!

CONNAL.

Bring me thy father's shield; the iron
shield of Rinval; that shield like the
full moon when it is darkened in the
sky.

CRIMORA.

That shield I bring, O Connal; but
it did not defend my father. By the
spear of Gauror he fell. Thou mayst
fall, O Connal!

CONNAL.

Fall indeed I may: But raise my
tomb, Crimora. Some stones, a mound
of earth, shall keep my memory.
Though fair thou art, my love, as the
light; more pleasant than the gale of
the hill; yet I will not stay. Raise my
tomb, Crimora.

CRIMORA,

Then give me those arms of light;
that sword, and that spear of steel. I
shall meet Dargo with thee, and aid my

lovely Connal. Farewell, ye rocks of
Ardven! ye deer! and ye streams of
the hill!—We shall return no more.
Our tombs are distant far.

V

Autumn is dark on the mountains;
grey mist rests on the hills. The
whirlwind is heard on the heath. Dark
rolls the river through the narrow plain.
A tree stands alone on the hill, and
marks the grave of Connal. The leaves
whirl round with the wind, and strew
the grave of the dead. At times are
seen here the ghosts of the deceased,
when the musing hunter alone stalks
slowly over the heath.

Who can reach the source of thy
race, O Connal? and who recount thy
Fathers? Thy family grew like an oak
on the mountain, which meeteth the
wind with its lofty head. But now it
is torn from the earth. Who shall supply
the place of Connal?

Here was the din of arms; and
here the groans of the dying. Mournful
are the wars of Fingal! O Connal!

it was here thou didst fall. Thine arm
was like a storm; thy sword, a beam
of the sky; thy height, a rock on the
plain; thine eyes, a furnace of fire.
Louder than a storm was thy voice,
when thou confoundedst the field. Warriors
fell by thy sword, as the thistle by
the staff of a boy.

Dargo the mighty came on, like a
cloud of thunder. His brows were contracted
and dark. His eyes like two
caves in a rock. Bright rose their
swords on each side; dire was the clang
of their steel.

The daughter of Rinval was near;
Crimora, bright in the armour of man;
her hair loose behind, her bow in her
hand. She followed the youth to the
war, Connal her much beloved. She
drew the string on Dargo; but erring
pierced her Connal. He falls like an
oak on the plain; like a rock from the
shaggy hill. What shall she do, hapless
maid!—He bleeds; her Connal dies.
All the night long she cries, and all the
day, O Connal, my love, and my
friend! With grief the sad mourner
died.

Earth here incloseth the loveliest
pair on the hill. The grass grows between
the stones of their tomb; I sit in
the mournful shade. The wind sighs
through the grass; and their memory

rushes on my mind. Undisturbed you
now sleep together; in the tomb of the
mountain you rest alone.

VI

Son of the noble Fingal, Oscian,
Prince of men! what tears run down
the cheeks of age? what shades thy
mighty soul?

Memory, son of Alpin, memory
wounds the aged. Of former times are
my thoughts; my thoughts are of the
noble Fingal. The race of the king return
into my mind, and wound me with
remembrance.

One day, returned from the sport of
the mountains, from pursuing the sons
of the hill, we covered this heath with
our youth. Fingal the mighty was here,
and Oscur, my son, great in war. Fair
on our sight from the sea, at once, a
virgin came. Her breast was like the
snow of one night. Her cheek like the
bud of the rose. Mild was her blue
rolling eye: but sorrow was big in her
heart.

Fingal renowned in war! she cries,
sons of the king, preserve me! Speak secure,
replies the king, daughter of beauty,
speak: our ear is open to all: our
swords redress the injured. I fly from
Ullin, she cries, from Ullin famous in
war. I fly from the embrace of him
who would debase my blood. Cremor,
the friend of men, was my father; Cremor
the Prince of Inverne.

Fingal's younger sons arose; Carryl
expert in the bow; Fillan beloved of
the fair; and Fergus first in the race.
—Who from the farthest Lochlyn?
who to the seas of Molochasquir? who
dares hurt the maid whom the sons of
Fingal guard? Daughter of beauty, rest
secure; rest in peace, thou fairest of women.

Far in the blue distance of the deep,
some spot appeared like the back of the
ridge—wave. But soon the ship increased
on our sight. The hand of Ullin drew
her to land. The mountains trembled
as he moved. The hills shook at his
steps. Dire rattled his armour around
him. Death and destruction were in his
eyes. His stature like the roe of Morven.
He moved in the lightning of
steel.

Our warriors fell before him,
like the field before the reapers. Fingal's
three sons he bound. He plunged
his sword into the fair—one's breast.

She fell as a wreath of snow before the
sun in spring. Her bosom heaved in
death; her soul came forth in blood.
Oscur my son came down; the
mighty in battle descended. His armour
rattled as thunder; and the lightning of
his eyes was terrible. There, was the
clashing of swords; there, was the voice
of steel. They struck and they thrust;
they digged for death with their swords.
But death was distant far, and delayed
to come. The sun began to decline;
and the cow–herd thought of home.
Then Oscur's keen steel found the heart
of Ullin. He fell like a mountain–oak
covered over with glittering frost: He
shone like a rock on the plain.—Here
the daughter of beauty lieth; and
here the bravest of men. Here one
day ended the fair and the valiant.
Here rest the pursuer and the pursued.

Son of Alpin! the woes of the aged
are many: their tears are for the past.
This raised my sorrow, warriour; memory
awaked my grief. Oscur my
son was brave; but Oscur is now no
more. Thou hast heard my grief, O
son of Alpin; forgive the tears of the
aged.

VII

Why openest thou afresh the spring of
my grief, O son of Alpin, inquiring
how Oscur fell? My eyes are blind with
tears; but memory beams on my heart.
How can I relate the mournful death of
the head of the people! Prince of the
warriours, Oscur my son, shall I see thee
no more!

He fell as the moon in a storm; as
the sun from the midst of his course,
when clouds rise from the waste of the
waves, when the blackness of the storm
inwraps the rocks of Ardannider. I, like
an ancient oak on Morven, I moulder
alone in my place. The blast hath lopped
my branches away; and I tremble
at the wings of the north. Prince of
the warriours, Oscur my son! shall I see
thee no more!

DERMID

DERMID and Oscur were one: They
reaped the battle together. Their
friendship was strong as their steel; and
death walked between them to the field.
They came on the foe like two rocks
falling from the brows of Ardven. Their
swords were stained with the blood of
the valiant: warriours fainted at their

names. Who was a match for Oscur,
but Dermid? and who for Dermid, but
Oscur?

THEY killed mighty Dargo in the
field; Dargo before invincible. His
daughter was fair as the morn; mild
as the beam of night. Her eyes, like
two stars in a shower: her breath, the
gale of spring: her breasts, as the
new fallen snow floating on the moving heath.
The warriors saw her, and loved; their
souls were fixed on the maid. Each
loved her, as his fame; each must
possess her or die. But her soul was fixed
on Oscur; my son was the youth of
her love. She forgot the blood of her
father; and loved the hand that slew
him.

Son of Oscian, said Dermid, I love;
O Oscur, I love this maid. But her
soul cleaveth unto thee; and nothing
can heal Dermid. Here, pierce this
bosom, Oscur; relieve me, my friend,
with thy sword.

My sword, son of Morny, shall never
be stained with the blood of Dermid.

Who then is worthy to slay me, O
Oscur son of Oscian? Let not my life
pass away unknown. Let none but Oscur
slay me. Send me with honour to
the grave, and let my death be renowned.
Dermid, make use of thy sword;

son of Moray, wield thy steel. Would
that I fell with thee! that my death
came from the hand of Dermid!

They fought by the brook of the
mountain; by the streams of Branno.
Blood tinged the silvery stream, and
crudled round the mossy stones. Dermid
the graceful fell; fell, and smiled in
death.

And fallest thou, son of Morny;
fallest, thou by Oscur's hand! Dermid
invincible in war, thus do I see thee fall!
—He went, and returned to the maid
whom he loved; returned, but she perceived
his grief.

Why that gloom, son of Oscian?
what shades thy mighty soul?

Though once renowned for the bow,
O maid, I have lost my fame. Fixed on
a tree by the brook of the hill, is the
shield of Gormur the brave, whom in
battle I slew. I have wasted the day
in vain, nor could my arrow pierce it.

Let me try, son Oscian, the skill
of Dargo's daughter. My hands were
taught the bow: my father delighted in
my skill.

She went. He stood behind the
shield. Her arrow flew and pierced his
breast[A].

Fragments Of Ancient Poetry

[Footnote A: Nothing was held by the ancient Highlanders more essential to their glory, than to die by the hand of some person worthy or renowned. This was the occasion of Oscur's contriving to be slain by his mistress, now that he was weary of life. In those early times suicide was utterly unknown among that people, and no traces of it are found in the old poetry. Whence the translator suspects the account that follows of the daughter of Dargo killing herself, to be the interpolation of some later Bard.]

Blessed be that hand of snow; and
blessed thy bow of yew! I fall resolved
on death: and who but the daughter of
Dargo was worthy to slay me? Lay me
in the earth, my fair–one; lay me by
the side of Dermid.

Oscur! I have the blood, the soul
of the mighty Dargo. Well pleased I
can meet death. My sorrow I can end
thus.—She pierced her white bosom
with steel. She fell; she trembled; and
died.

By the brook of the hill their graves
are laid; a birch's unequal shade covers
their tomb. Often on their green earthen
tombs the branchy sons of the mountain
feed, when mid–day is all in flames,
and silence is over all the hills.

VIII

By the side of a rock on the hill, beneath
the aged trees, old Oscian
sat on the moss; the last of the race of
Fingal. Sightless are his aged eyes;
his beard is waving in the wind. Dull
through the leafless trees he heard the
voice of the north. Sorrow revived in
his soul: he began and lamented the
dead.

How hast thou fallen like an oak,
with all thy branches round thee! Where
is Fingal the King? where is Oscur my
son? where are all my race? Alas! in
the earth they lie. I feel their tombs
with my hands. I hear the river below
murmuring hoarsely over the stones.
What dost thou, O river, to me? Thou
bringest back the memory of the past.

The race of Fingal stood on thy
banks, like a wood in a fertile soil.
Keen were their spears of steel. Hardy
was he who dared to encounter their
rage. Fillan the great was there. Thou
Oscur wert there, my son! Fingal himself
was there, strong in the grey locks
of years. Full rose his sinewy limbs;
and wide his shoulders spread. The
unhappy met with his arm, when the
pride of his wrath arose.

The son of Morny came; Gaul, the
tallest of men. He stood on the hill like
an oak; his voice was like the streams of
the hill. Why reigneth alone, he cries,
the son of the mighty Corval? Fingal is
not strong to save: he is no support for
the people. I am strong as a storm in
the ocean; as a whirlwind on the hill.
Yield, son of Corval; Fingal, yield to
me.

Oscur stood forth to meet him;
my son would meet the foe. But Fingal
came in his strength, and smiled at
the vaunter's boast. They threw their
arms round each other; they struggled
on the plain. The earth is ploughed with
their heels. Their bones crack as the boat
on the ocean, when it leaps from wave to
wave. Long did they toil; with night,
they fell on the sounding plain; as two
oaks, with their branches mingled, fall
crashing from the hill. The tall son
of Morny is bound; the aged overcame.

Fair with her locks of gold, her
smooth neck, and her breasts of snow;
fair, as the spirits of the hill when at
silent noon they glide along the heath;
fair, as the rainbow of heaven; came
Minvane the maid. Fingal! She softly
saith, loose me my brother Gaul.
Loose me the hope of my race, the terror
of all but Fingal. Can I, replies the
King, can I deny the lovely daughter

34

of the hill? take thy brother, O Minvane,
thou fairer than the snow of the
north!

Such, Fingal! were thy words; but
thy words I hear no more. Sightless
I sit by thy tomb. I hear the wind in
the wood; but no more I hear my
friends. The cry of the hunter is over.
The voice of war is ceased.

IX

Thou askest, fair daughter of the
isles! whose memory is preserved
in these tombs? The memory of Ronnan
the bold, and Connan the chief of
men; and of her, the fairest of maids,
Rivine the lovely and the good. The
wing of time is laden with care. Every
moment hath woes of its own. Why
seek we our grief from afar? or give our
tears to those of other times? But thou
commanded, and I obey, O fair daughter
of the isles!

Conar was mighty in war. Caul
was the friend of strangers. His gates
were open to all; midnight darkened
not on his barred door. Both lived upon

the sons of the mountains. Their bow
was the support of the poor.

Connan was the image of Conar's
soul. Caul was renewed in Ronnan his
son. Rivine the daughter of Conar was
the love of Ronnan; her brother Connan
was his friend. She was fair as the
harvest—moon setting in the seas of
Molochasquir. Her soul was settled on
Ronnan; the youth was the dream of her
nights.

Rivine, my love! says Ronnan, I go
to my king in Norway[A]. A year and
a day shall bring me back. Wilt thou
be true to Ronnan?

[Footnote A: Supposed to be Fergus II. This fragment is reckoned not
altogether so ancient as most of the rest.]

Ronnan! a year and a day I will
spend in sorrow. Ronnan, behave like
a man, and my soul shall exult in thy
valour. Connan my friend, says Ronnan,
wilt thou preserve Rivine thy sister?
Durstan is in love with the maid;
and soon shall the sea bring the stranger
to our coast.

Ronnan, I will defend: Do thou
securely go.—He went. He returned
on his day. But Durstan returned
before him.

Give me thy daughter, Conar, says

Durstan; or fear and feel my power.

He who dares attempt my sister, says
Connan, must meet this edge of steel.
Unerring in battle is my arm: my
sword, as the lightning of heaven.

Ronnan the warriour came; and
much he threatened Durstan.

But, saith Euran the servant of
gold, Ronnan! by the gate of the north
shall Durstan this night carry thy fair–one
away. Accursed, answers Ronnan, be this arm if death meet him not
there.

Connan! saith Euran, this night
shall the stranger carry thy sister away.
My sword shall meet him, replies Connan,
and he shall lie low on earth.
.

The friends met by night, and they
fought. Blood and sweat ran down
their limbs as water on the mossy rock.
Connan falls; and cries, O Durstan,
be favourable to Rivine!—And is it my
friend, cries Ronnan, I have slain? O
Connan! I knew thee not.

He went, and he fought with Durstan.
Day began to rise on the combat,
when fainting they fell, and expired.
Rivine came out with the morn;
and—O what detains my Ronnan!
—She saw him lying pale in his blood;
and her brother lying pale by his side.

What could she say: what could she
do? her complaints were many and vain.
She opened this grave for the warriours;
and fell into it herself, before it
was closed; like the sun snatched away
in a storm.

Thou hast heard this tale of grief,
O fair daughter of the isles! Rivine was
fair as thyself: shed on her grave a
tear.

X

It is night; and I am alone, forlorn
on the hill of storms. The wind is
heard in the mountain. The torrent
shrieks down the rock. No hut receives
me from the rain; forlorn on the hill of
winds.

Rise, moon! from behind thy
clouds; stars of the night, appear!
Lead me, some light, to the place where
my love rests from the toil of the chase!
his bow near him, unstrung; his dogs
panting around him. But here I must
sit alone, by the rock of the mossy
stream. The stream and the wind

roar; nor can I hear the voice of my
love.

Why delayeth my Shalgar, why the
son of the hill, his promise? Here is
the rock; and the tree; and here the
roaring stream. Thou promisedst with
night to be here. Ah! whither is my
Shalgar gone? With thee I would fly
my father; with thee, my brother of
pride. Our race have long been foes;
but we are not foes, O Shalgar!

Cease a little while, O wind! stream,
be thou silent a while! let my voice be
heard over the heath; let my wanderer
hear me. Shalgar! it is I who call. Here
is the tree, and the rock. Shalgar, my
love! I am here. Why delayest thou
thy coming? Alas! no answer.

Lo! the moon appeareth. The
flood is bright in the vale. The rocks
are grey on the face of the hill. But
I see him not on the brow; his dogs
before him tell not that he is coming.
Here I must sit alone.

But who are these that lie beyond
me on the heath? Are they my love
and my brother?—Speak to me, O my
friends! they answer not. My soul is
tormented with fears.—Ah! they are
dead. Their swords are red from the
fight. O my brother! my brother!
why hast thou slain my Shalgar? why,

O Shalgar! hast thou slain my brother?
Dear were ye both to me! speak to me;
hear my voice, sons of my love! But
alas! they are silent; silent for ever!
Cold are their breast of clay!

Oh! from the rock of the hill;
from the top of the mountain of winds,
speak ye ghosts of the dead! speak,
and I will not be afraid.—Whither
are ye gone to rest? In what cave of
the hill shall I find you?

I sit in my grief. I wait for morning
in my tears. Rear the tomb, ye
friends of the dead; but close it not
till I come. My life flieth away like a
dream: why should I stay behind?
Here shall I rest with my friends by the
stream of the founding rock. When
night comes on the hill: when the wind
is up on the heath; my ghost shall stand
in the wind, and mourn the death of
my friends. The hunter shall hear
from his booth. He shall fear, but
love my voice. For sweet shall my voice
be for my friends; for pleasant were
they both to me.

XI

Fragments Of Ancient Poetry

Sad! I am sad indeed: nor small my
cause of woe!—Kirmor, thou hast
lost no son; thou hast lost no daughter
of beauty. Connar the valiant lives;
and Annir the fairest of maids. The
boughs of thy family flourish, O Kirmor!
but Armyn is the last of his
race.

Rise, winds of autumn, rise; blow
upon the dark heath! streams of the
mountains, roar! howl, ye tempests,
in the trees! walk through broken
clouds, O moon! show by intervals thy
pale face! bring to my mind that sad
night, when all my children fell; when
Arindel the mighty fell; when Daura
the lovely died.

Daura, my daughter! thou wert
fair; fair as the moon on the hills of
Jura; white as the driven snow; sweet as
the breathing gale. Armor renowned in
war came, and fought Daura's love; he
was not long denied; fair was the hope
of their friends.

Earch son of Odgal repined; for
his brother was slain by Armor. He
came disguised like a son of the sea:
fair was his skiff on the wave; white
his locks of age; calm his serious brow.
Fairest of women, he said, lovely daughter
of Armyn! a rock not distant in
the sea, bears a tree on its side; red

shines the fruit afar. There Armor
waiteth for Daura. I came to fetch
his love. Come, fair daughter of Armyn!

She went; and she called on Armor.
Nought answered, but the son of the
rock. Armor, my love! my love!
why tormentest thou me with fear?
come, graceful son of Arduart, come;
it is Daura who calleth thee!—Earch
the traitor fled laughing to the land.
She lifted up her voice, and cried for
her brother and her father. Arindel!
Armyn! none to relieve your Daura?

Her voice came over the sea. Arindel
my son descended from the hill;
rough in the spoils of the chace. His
arrows rattled by his side; his bow was
in his hand; five grey dogs attended
his steps. He saw fierce Earch on the
shore; he seized and bound him to an
oak. Thick fly the thongs of the hide
around his limbs; he loads the wind
with his groans.

Arindel ascends the surgy deep in
his boat, to bring Daura to the land.
Armor came in his wrath, and let fly
the grey–feathered shaft. It sung; it
sunk in thy heart, O Arindel my son!
for Earch the traitor thou diedst. What
is thy grief, O Daura, when round
thy feet is poured thy brother's blood!

The boat is broken in twain by the

waves. Armor plunges into the sea, to
rescue his Daura or die. Sudden a blast
from the hill comes over the waves.
He sunk, and he rose no more.

Alone, on the sea–beat rock, my
daughter was heard to complain. Frequent
and loud were her cries; nor
could her father relieve her. All
night I stood on the shore. All night I
heard her cries. Loud was the wind;
and the rain beat hard on the side of the
mountain. Before morning appeared,
her voice was weak. It died away, like
the evening–breeze among the grass of
the rocks. Spent with grief she expired.
O lay me soon by her side.

When the storms of the mountain
come; when the north lifts the waves
on high; I sit by the sounding shore,
and look on the fatal rock. Often by
the setting moon I see the ghosts of
my children. Indistinct, they walk in
mournful conference together. Will
none of you speak to me?—But they
do not regard their father.

XII

RYNO, ALPIN.

RYNO

The wind and the rain are over:
calm is the noon of day. The
clouds are divided in heaven. Over
the green hills flies the inconstant sun.
Red through the stony vale comes
down the stream of the hill. Sweet are
thy murmurs, O stream! but more
sweet is the voice I hear. It is the voice
of Alpin the son of the song, mourning
for the dead. Bent is his head of age,
and red his tearful eye. Alpin, thou
son of the song, why alone on the silent
hill? why complainest thou, as a
blast in the wood; as a wave on the
lonely shore?

ALPIN.

My tears, O Ryno! are for the dead;
my voice, for the inhabitants of the
grave. Tall thou art on the hill; fair
among the sons of the plain. But thou
shalt fall like Morar; and the mourner
shalt sit on thy tomb. The hills shall
know thee no more; thy bow shall lie in
the hall, unstrung.

Thou wert swift, O Morar! as a
doe on the hill; terrible as a meteor of
fire. Thy wrath was as the storm of
December. Thy sword in battle, as
lightning in the field. Thy voice was

44

like a stream after rain; like thunder
on distant hills. Many fell by thy
arm; they were consumed in the flames
of thy wrath.

But when thou returnedst from war,
how peaceful was thy brow! Thy face
was like the sun after rain; like the
moon in the silence of night; calm as
the breast of the lake when the loud
wind is laid.

Narrow is thy dwelling now; dark
the place of thine abode. With three
steps I compass thy grave, O thou who
wast so great before! Four stones with
their heads of moss are the only memorial
of thee. A tree with scarce a leaf,
long grass which whistles in the wind,
mark to the hunter's eye the grave of
the mighty Morar. Morar! thou art
low indeed. Thou hast no mother to
mourn thee; no maid with her tears of
love. Dead is she that brought thee
forth. Fallen is the daughter of Morglan.

Who on his staff is this? who is this,
whose head is white with age, whose
eyes are red with tears, who quakes
at every step?—It is thy father, O
Morar! the father of none but thee.
He heard of thy fame in battle; he heard
of foes dispersed. He heard of Morar's
fame; why did he not hear of his
wound? Weep, thou father of Morar!
weep; but thy son heareth thee not.

Deep is the sleep of the dead; low their
pillow of dust. No more shall he hear
thy voice; no more shall he awake at
thy call. When shall it be morn in the
grave, to bid the slumberer awake?

Farewell, thou bravest of men!
thou conqueror in the field! but the field
shall see thee no more; nor the dark
wood be lightened with the splendor of
thy steel. Thou hast left no son.
But the song shall preserve thy name.
Future times shall hear of thee; they
shall hear of the fallen Morar.

XIII

[Footnote: This is the opening of the epic poem mentioned in the preface.
The two following fragments are parts of some episodes of the same work.]

Cuchlaid sat by the wall; by the
tree of the rustling leaf.

[Footnote: The aspen or poplar tree]

His spear leaned against the mossy rock.
His shield lay by him on the grass.
Whilst he thought on the mighty Carbre
whom he slew in battle, the scout of
the ocean came, Moran the son of Fithil.

Rise, Cuchulaid, rise! I see the ships
of Garve. Many are the foe, Cuchulaid;
many the sons of Lochlyn.

Moran! thou ever tremblest; thy
fears increase the foe. They are the
ships of the Desert of hills arrived to assist
Cuchulaid.

I saw their chief, says Moran, tall as
a rock of ice. His spear is like that fir;
his shield like the rising moon. He sat
upon a rock on the shore, as a grey
cloud upon the hill. Many, mighty
man! I said, many are our heroes;
Garve, well art thou named,
many are the sons of our king.

[Footnote: Garve sigifies a man of great size.]

He answered like a wave on the
rock; who is like me here? The valiant
live not with me; they go to the
earth from my hand. The king of the
Desert of hills alone can fight with
Garve. Once we wrestled on the hill.
Our heels overturned the wood. Rocks
fell from their place, and rivulets changed
their course. Three days we strove
together; heroes stood at a distance,
and feared. On the fourth, the King
saith that I fell; but Garve saith, he
stood. Let Cuchulaid yield to him that
is strong as a storm.

No. I will never yield to man.
Cuchulaid will conquer or die. Go,
Moran, take my spear; strike the shield
of Caithbait which hangs before the
gate. It never rings in peace. My heroes
shall hear on the hill,—

XIV

DUCHOMMAR, MORNA.

DUCHOMMAR.

[Footnote: The signification of the names in this fragment are;
Dubhchomar, a black well–shaped man. Muirne or Morna, a woman beloved
by all. Cormac–cairbre, an unequalled and rough warriour. Cromleach,
a crooked hill. Mugruch, a surly gloomy man. Tarman, thunder. Moinie,
soft in temper and person.]

Morna, thou fairest of women,
daughter of Cormac–Carbre!
why in the circle of stones, in the cave
of the rock, alone? The stream murmureth
hoarsely. The blast groaneth
in the aged tree. The lake is troubled
before thee. Dark are the clouds of
the sky. But thou art like snow on
the heath. Thy hair like a thin cloud
of gold on the top of Cromleach. Thy
breasts like two smooth rocks on the hill

which is seen from the stream of Brannuin.
Thy arms, as two white pillars
in the hall of Fingal.

MORNA.

Whence the son of Mugruch, Duchommar
the most gloomy of men? Dark
are thy brows of terror. Red thy rolling
eyes. Does Garve appear on the
sea? What of the foe, Duchommar?

DUCHOMMAR.

From the hill I return, O Morna,
from the hill of the flying deer. Three
have I slain with my bow; three with
my panting dogs. Daughter of Cormac–Carbre,
I love thee as my soul. I
have slain a deer for thee. High was
his branchy head; and fleet his feet of
wind.

MORNA.

Gloomy son of Mugruch, Duchommar!
I love thee not: hard is thy heart
of rock; dark thy terrible brow. But
Cadmor the son of Tarman, thou art
the love of Morna! thou art like a sunbeam
on the hill, in the day of the
gloomy storm. Sawest thou the son of
Tarman, lovely on the hill of the chace?
Here the daughter of Cormac–Carbre
waiteth the coming of Cadmor.

DUCHOMMAR.

And long shall Morna wait. His
blood is on my sword. I met him by
the mossy stone, by the oak of the noisy
stream. He fought; but I slew him;
his blood is on my sword. High on
the hill I will raise his tomb, daughter
of Cormac–Carbre. But love thou the
son of Mugruch; his arm is strong as a
storm.

MORNA.

And is the son of Tarman fallen;
the youth with the breast of snow! the
first in the chase of the hill; the foe
of the sons of the ocean!—Duchommar,
thou art gloomy indeed; cruel is
thy arm to me.—But give me that
sword, son of Mugruch; I love the
blood of Cadmor.

[He gives her the sword, with which she instantly stabs him.]

DUCHOMMAR.

Daughter of Cormac–Carbre, thou
hast pierced Duchommar! the sword is
cold in my breast; thou hast killed the
son of Mugruch. Give me to Moinic
the maid; for much she loved Duchommar.
My tomb she will raise on the
hill; the hunter shall see it, and praise
me.—But draw the sword from my
side, Morna; I feel it cold.—

50

[Upon her coming near him, he stabs her. As she fell, she plucked a stone from the side of the cave, and placed it betwixt them, that his blood might not be mingled with hers.]

XV

[1]Where is Gealchossa my love, the
daughter of Tuathal–Teachvar?
I left her in the hall of the plain, when I
fought with the hairy Ulfadha. Return
soon, she said, O Lamderg! for
here I wait in sorrow. Her white breaft
rose with sighs; her cheek was wet
with tears. But she cometh not to meet
Lamderg; or sooth his soul after battle.
Silent is the hall of joy; I hear not
the voice of the singer. Brann does
not shake his chains at the gate, glad
at the coming of his master. Where
is Gealchossa my love, the daughter of
Tuathal–Teachvar?

[Footnote: The signification of the names in this fragment are;
Gealchossack, white–legged. Tuathal–Teachtmhar, the surly, but fortunate
man. Lambhdearg, bloodyhand. Ulfadba, long beard. Fichios, the conqueror
of men.]

Lamderg! says Firchios son of Aydon,
Gealchossa may be on the hill;

she and her chosen maids pursuing the
flying deer.

Firchios! no noise I hear. No
sound in the wood of the hill. No
deer fly in my sight; no panting dog
pursueth. I see not Gealchossa my
love; fair as the full moon setting on
the hills of Cromleach. Go, Firchios!
go to Allad, the grey–haired son of
the rock. He liveth in the circle of
stones; he may tell of Gealchossa.

[Footnote: Allad is plainly a Druid consulted on this occasion.]

Allad! saith Firchios, thou who
dwellest in the rock; thou who tremblest
alone; what saw thine eyes of
age?

I saw, answered Allad the old, Ullin the son of Carbre: He came like a
cloud from the hill; he hummed a surly
song as he came, like a storm in
leafless wood. He entered the hall of
the plain. Lamderg, he cried, most
dreadful of men! fight, or yield to Ullin.
Lamderg, replied Gealchoffa,
Lamderg is not here: he fights the
hairy Ulfadha; mighty man, he is not
here. But Lamderg never yields; he
will fight the son of Carbre. Lovely art
thou, O daughter of Tuathal–Teachvar!
said Ullin. I carry thee to the
house of Carbre; the valiant shall have
Gealchossa. Three days from the top
of Cromleach will I call Lamderg to

fight. The fourth, you belong to Ullin,
if Lamderg die, or fly my sword.

Allad! peace to thy dreams!—found
the horn, Firchios!—Ullin may
hear, and meet me on the top of Cromleach.

Lamderg rushed on like a storm.
On his spear he leaped over rivers. Few
were his strides up the hill. The rocks
fly back from his heels; loud crashing
they bound to the plain. His armour,
his buckler rung. He hummed a surly
song, like the noise of the falling
stream. Dark as a cloud he stood above;
his arms, like meteors, shone.
From the summit of the hill, he rolled
a rock. Ullin heard in the hall of
Carbre.—

Printed in the United States
53489LVS00004B/10